The Wonders of the Color Wheel

by CHARLES GHIGNA   illustrated by AG JATKOWSKA

PICTURE WINDOW BOOKS
a capstone imprint

Finding colors is an art.
The COLOR WHEEL is where we start!

3

Three bright colors for me and you.
Primary colors: **RED**, YELLOW, **BLUE!**

RED is an apple,

YELLOW, the sun.

6

BLUE is the sky when the day has begun.

Mix primary colors, and what do you get?
Secondary colors:
ORANGE, GREEN, and **VIOLET**.

BLUE and YELLOW turn into GREEN,

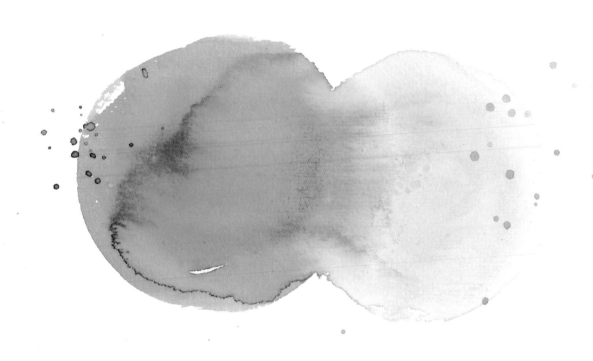

like a grassy hillside scene.

ORANGE comes from **RED** and YELLOW.

An ORANGE pumpkin
makes a
funny fellow.

VIOLET comes from RED and BLUE.

VIOLET is a purple hue.

We see colors passing by
every morning in the sky.

The sky is **BLUE**. The clouds are **WHITE**.

The sky turns **BLACK** with each new night.

BLACK and WHITE turn into GRAY,

like a cloudy, rainy day.

After rain comes the YELLOW sun.

A perfect time for picnic fun!

Early morning, late at night—

colors paint the world so bright!

Colors are a lot of fun.
Do you have a favorite one?

PRIMARY COLORS

RED   YELLOW   BLUE

SECONDARY COLORS

ORANGE   GREEN   VIOLET

READ MORE

Harris, Nancy. *Comparing Colors.* Colors. Chicago: Raintree, 2008.

Kiely, Orla. *Colors.* New York: Henry Hot and Co., 2012.

Dardik, Helen, illus. *Pantone Colors.* New York: Abrams Appleseed, 2012.

INTERNET SITES

FactHound offers a safe, fun way to find Internet sites related to this book. All of the sites on FactHound have been researched by our staff.

Here's all you do:

Visit *www.facthound.com*

Type in this code: 9781404883079

 Check out projects, games and lots more at
www.capstonekids.com

Look for all the books in the series:

For Charlotte and Christopher.

Thanks to our adviser for his expertise, research, and advice:
Terry Flaherty, PhD, Professor of English
Minnesota State University, Mankato

Editor: Shelly Lyons
Designer: Ashlee Suker
Art Director: Nathan Gassman
Production Specialist: Laura Manthe
The illustrations in this book were created digitally.

Picture Window Books are published by Capstone,
1710 Roe Crest Drive, North Mankato, Minnesota 56003
www.capstonepub.com

Library of Congress Cataloging-in-Publication Data
Ghigna, Charles.
The wonders of the color wheel / by Charles Ghigna ; illustrated by
Ag Jatkowska.
pages cm. — (My little school house)
Summary: "Introduces primary and secondary colors through fun, poetic
text."— Provided by publisher.
Audience: K to grade 3.
ISBN 978-1-4048-8307-9 (library binding)
ISBN 978-1-4048-8311-6 (board book)
ISBN 978-1-4795-1897-5 (ebook pdf)
1. Color—Juvenile literature. I. Jatkowska, Ag, illustrator. II. Title.

QC495.5.G45 2014
535.6—dc23   2013007627